Buddhist Beliefs & Principles

Understanding the Basic Principles of Buddhism and How to Incorporate Buddhism into Your Life

~ Buddhism for Beginners ~

by Chaya Rao

Table of Contents

Introduction

Buddhism is a religion that is comprised of various different traditions, teachings, and practices. The religion was originally founded by Siddhartha Gautama, whom his followers refer to as "Buddha," which can be translated into 'the enlightened one.'

You may already be aware of some of the singular and more mainstream concepts of the religion, such as meditation. However, Buddhism is much, much more than just meditation, and offers the potential for a deep understanding of life and its meaning, suffering, and enlightenment.

Through this book, you will come to understand and appreciate the basics of Buddhism; you will learn how to easily incorporate the Buddhist principles into your own everyday life; and you will realize how adopting the Buddhist mindset can dramatically improve your sense of happiness and wellbeing.

Let's get started!

Chapter 1: The Role of Doctrine and The Eightfold Path

Before we explore and go deeper in Buddhism's main principles, let's start off with the role of doctrine, whereby the Great Buddha stressed that none of his teachings be followed blindly, without proper contemplation. The increasing scientific development in the world of today has equipped us with what we need in order to verify different facts, teachings, and whatnot. And with Buddhism's encouragement to use a scientific microscope, the religion is increasingly gaining popularity.

One thing to note, however, is that this permission or encouragement to examine the teachings of Buddha in no way means that any of the primary aspects of the religion are optional. A complete follower of the religion needs to incorporate each and every aspect.

This book is meant to be a guide for the most important elements of Buddhism. And when it comes to important elements, the discussion of Eightfold Path is never far away.

After Buddha gained enlightenment, he took some time to think about how to preach this to others around him. When he gave his first sermon, he stressed how humans are plagued with suffering, what suffering really is, and how we can liberate ourselves from such suffering. The discussion of liberation gave birth to the Eightfold Path, which is basically a way of escaping the suffering. While these eight points are listed numerically, that doesn't mean that one is more important than another. It is more of holistic manual that must be exercised and kept in consideration at all times, simultaneously.

The Eightfold Path includes:

1. Right View
2. Right Intention
3. Right Speech
4. Right Action
5. Right Livelihood
6. Right Effort
7. Right Mindfulness
8. Right Concentration

Despite the fact that it consists of eight points, the Right View is the most-discussed aspect, as it lays the foundation for the rest of the points to come. So what exactly is this Right View? Right View is associated with wisdom. It is about seeing things as they are. It is also very closely associated with the Four Noble Truths, which we will discuss after this.

In the book, 'The Heart of the Buddha's Teaching,' Zen teacher Thich Nhat Hanh says,

"Our happiness and the happiness of those around us depend on our degree of Right View. Touching reality deeply -- knowing what is going on inside and outside of ourselves -- is the way to liberate ourselves from the suffering that is caused by wrong perceptions. Right View is not an ideology, a system, or even a path. It is the insight we have into the

reality of life, a living insight that fills us with understanding, peace, and love."

Right Intention refers to wanting good for everyone around us, it means wanting to free humanity from the suffering that it has to bear. Right Action means actually exercising such intentions. See how they go together? So in the context of real life, if you see someone who is having a hard time crossing the street, the right intention would be wanting to help that person cross the road, while right action would involve you actually going and doing it.

Right speech also comes with right action as it involves doing good to those around you through both your hands and tongue. It involves speaking the truth, while leaving the side of falsehood.

The rest of the eight aspects are directed toward the same goal: being a good, enlightened human being as a whole. As you read through this book, you will realize that the roots of Buddhism are quite easily connected to being a spiritual being, from whom others can learn and benefit.

According to Walpola Rahula, *"Practically the whole teaching of the Buddha, to which he devoted himself during 45 years, deals in some way or other with this [Eightfold] path."*

So, what this Eightfold Path really leads you toward is wisdom or prajna. The 8 objectives provide the necessary guidance for you to stay on track. Remember, this is not about self improvement from the selfish perspective of only benefiting yourself. There is no room for selfishness in Buddhism.

Being honest, speaking what is true, doing what is good, and helping others – these are actions that, if incorporated into our daily lives, can lead us to true wisdom.

Again, the teachings are not imposed on anyone, but are meant to be examined through one's own experiences in order to be exercised and incorporated into daily routine.

Chapter 2: The Four Noble Truths

If there is one aspect of Buddhism that describes the whole religion, it is the Four Noble Truths. These were revealed by Buddha in his first sermon, and they became the building blocks of Buddhism as we know it today. These truths are:

The truth of suffering (dukkha)

The word dukkha represents anything that is conditional, anything that passes or is not permanent. The exact translation of the first Noble Truth is 'life is suffering.' This may seem a little odd at first, especially if you are new to Buddhism. However, Buddha went on to explain what this truth is all about. The idea behind it is to understand the fact that we are not immortal, nor are any of our feelings, or suffering. Everything that starts and has an end is dukkha, be it happiness, sadness, grief, or anything else for that matter. Buddha stressed that we must understand 'self' before we consider the concepts of life and death.

The truth of the cause of suffering (samudaya)

The second truth is the reason we suffer, and that is because we crave what we do not have. This is a universal truth – our wants are unlimited. As soon as we have something, we want more. We look toward other people's plates and we tend to envy. We wish to acquire what we do not have, while disregarding what we do have. This is jealousy, and there are few things worse than jealousy.

Buddha taught that by going after such worldly things, we lose ourselves and our path. From material things to opinions, ideas, and whatnot, we get so involved in ourselves that when things do not go as we wish them to, we grieve. That, Buddha stresses, is what leads to suffering.

The lesson we can learn here is quite obvious, and one that we can all relate to. Even today, when we see people who have more, we wonder why we don't. We don't look toward those with less and give thanks, but always go for more and thus are never really satisfied. By eliminating this preoccupation, we can relieve ourselves and gain true bliss.

The truth of the end of suffering (nirhodha)

Having explained what suffering is and what causes it, Buddha then taught how to cure it. The cure, he said, could be found through practice. By making ourselves stronger, and not giving in to our never-ending wants, we can reach the stage of enlightenment that will help us reach a state of Nirvana.

The idea is to keep on trying, to keep looking the other way and controlling ourselves when we are faced with our overwhelming desires. It may be the hardest thing we ever have to do, but it is the route to real liberation.

The truth of the path that frees us from suffering (magga)

By stressing over and over again on the concept that believing is not enough, Buddha taught that his teachings need be molded into a lifestyle. It is not enough to know and speak. You must exercise it. The path he taught is discussed above as the Eightfold Path.

Chapter 3: Tolerance

Another very important aspect of Buddhism is tolerance. Buddhism teaches a very wide scope of tolerance, which encompasses being tolerant of one another in daily affairs, being tolerant when faced with difficulties, and being tolerant when wrong is done to you.

Many prominent Buddhists consider tolerance to be the foremost principle of Buddha's teachings. They believe that the real bliss, the real happiness that humans strive for in their daily lives can truly be found when they exercise absolute tolerance. Hardships come, hardships go. What remains is the human spirit. Tolerance is seeing through all that is thrown at you without losing sight of the ultimate goal that you are moving toward.

What makes this aspect of Buddhism all the more important is that it overlaps with the message of peace and love that not just Buddhism but most religions around the world teach. Without tolerance, we would all be tearing each other apart instead of sitting down in an assembly that is full of representatives from every corner of the world.

In our everyday lives, tolerance involves facing difficulties and looking them in the eye. It involves not losing hope and always believing in yourself. Take the example of a situation in which you are faced with financial hardship. You have lost your job, your future prospects seem bleak, your romantic relationship is in jeopardy, and you feel as though there is no way out of such a disaster. Tolerance would involve acknowledging these matters and solving them calmly without losing heart, without giving up. It doesn't involve looking for a shortcut out or becoming desperate to make things better. Instead, only acceptance, perseverance, and a sense of peace will help you come out on top again.

The concept of tolerance moves from hardships to other human beings. If someone has done you wrong, for example someone who has cheated you, it is only natural to feel rage. However, Buddhism prohibits you from going after that someone with a mind full of revenge. Here, you are to exercise tolerance: you have to let it go. It may not be the easiest thing to do, but when it comes down to it, you must take a deep breath and just simply let go of it, remembering that it is not your job to even the score or impose justice.

And, it is not just tolerance for one another, but for other religions, as well. A very important and interesting aspect of Buddhism is that they are not concerned with labels such as 'Hindus,' 'Muslims,' or 'Christians.' All they are concerned with is their own teaching.

You can look back in history and struggle to find even one war that was fought in the name of Buddhism. Such is the way that this religion presents itself. It does not try to preach, nor convert. It doesn't hold many promotional activities, where it tries to reach out to people. You won't see any Buddhist on social media pushing their religious affiliations. What this tells you is that Buddhism is about being happy; it's about being content with yourself and what you have. It's not about getting more or converting people to get them to do more. Instead, it's about each individual playing their own role as a Buddhist.

From forgiving people for the wrong they have done to calmly accepting differing views in what might otherwise be a heated discussion, the scope of tolerance we can exercise in our everyday lives is very wide. However, if we are willing to learn, this could be the best lesson that we will ever come across. The idea of not losing one's patience and always striving to be better is not just something that can provide you with peace of mind, but it is something that can actually lead you to the ultimate success in life.

Chapter 4: Karma

Karma is a word that is thrown around quite often these days. It is construed as a universal, yet divine, justice system that holds you responsible for all of your actions. It's like the give respect, get respect rule. However, Buddhism takes a rather different stance on its meaning.

The word, in Sanskrit, means action. And so, unlike the conventional understanding of Karma as a result of an action, Buddhism defines Karma as the action itself, not the consequence. So, in Buddhism, when you carry out a particular willful action, it sets Karma in motion. The result is referred to as 'fruit.'

According to Buddhist Monk Thanissaro Bhikku, Karma "*acts in multiple feedback loops, with the present moment being shaped both by past and by present actions; present actions shape not only the future but also the present.*" What he means here is that not only is the past reflecting on the present, but the present is reflecting on itself and the future as well.

With Karma, you learn that if you believe your actions will go unnoticed and without repercussions, you are only fooling yourself. It teaches you that every step you take comes back to shape your life.

As per the famous scholar Walpola Rahula,

"The theory of karma should not be confused with so-called 'moral justice' or 'reward and punishment'. The idea of moral justice, or reward and punishment, arises out of the conception of a supreme being, a God, who sits in judgment, who is a law-giver and who decides what is right and wrong. The term 'justice' is ambiguous and dangerous, and in its name more harm than good is done to humanity. The theory of karma is the theory of cause and effect, of action and reaction; it is a natural law, which has nothing to do with the idea of justice or reward and punishment."

Karma is not just taught in Buddhism, but in most mainstream religions as well. In Islam, you are taught to do good to others in order to expect good to be done to you. The same goes for mischief. This is basically the same as Karma. It is teaching you that you cannot go around spreading trouble and then expect all your wishes to become true. It also teaches you that any of your actions that create a source of trouble for others will never go unnoticed.

Let's explain Karma with an example. Imagine finding out that your neighbors are going through a tough time. They don't have enough food to feed all mouths, and you are well aware of this situation. There is ample food in your house and you are more than able to help them, but for some selfish reason, you choose not to. The Karma here is that if you are engaged in such a selfish display, you will find out that when the tables have turned and you become the one in need of help, your neighbors would embody this selfish stance of yours, and help will not be coming.

What the concept of Karma implies is that you should be good to others so that they are, in turn, good to you. It is like give and take – the more you give, the more you take. It teaches you that you should avoid being selfish and feeling invulnerable. Humility coincides with the concept of Karma, stating clearly that nobody is untouchable and that if you are a source of trouble for someone, you will have someone who is a source of trouble for you. Tit for tat.

Believing in Karma and shaping your life according to it involves not doing harm to others, as it would eventually come back to haunt you. It involves keeping in mind the eventual consequences of every move we make so that we ensure that it is not wrong or selfish. When we expect good from doing good, what do we do? We do good. It is as simple as that. In this way, it can be interpreted similarly to the "Golden Rule," which you are probably already familiar: "One should treat others as one would like others to treat oneself."

Chapter 5: Compassion

One thing Buddha quite specifically emphasized was enlightenment, something he believed to be crucial to the foundation of Buddhism. He believed that true enlightenment was formed by a combination of wisdom and compassion. According to him, these two travel side by side, as if they were two wings that help fly.

Convention dictates very different definitions of compassion and wisdom, two separate things that do not coincide. While compassion is shown as merely emotional, wisdom is shown as something merely intellectual. What this does is pit these two against each other, making us think that we cannot actually use our full intellect as long as we are emotional. So what we can assume is that compassion and wisdom cannot coexist. This is conventional thinking.

Buddhism takes a rather different route. Wisdom in Buddhism is about consciousness; it's about understanding what Buddha taught – something entirely different from the conventional meaning.

In Buddhism, it is said that wisdom and compassion are to be exercised together. Without one, there is no other. So, let's continue with compassion, which is discussed in far more detail. The word used for compassion is Buddhism is 'karuna.' Some translate it to sympathy, while it is also known as willingness to suffer in the place of others. It is about letting go of your own interests, and putting the interests of those around you first.

The concept of compassion or karuna is rather idealistic. It encourages you to eliminate suffering from wherever you see it. In practice, it may seem impossible, and really it is. However, Buddhism teaches you to try anyway. It teaches that if everyone tries their best, there will be no more suffering. It is about collectively being compassionate so that the world becomes a better place.

But you may ask what being compassionate has to do with being enlightened? Buddhism emphasizes that true enlightenment lies in realizing that there is no "you" and no "me," only "we." It stresses that by being compassionate and taking into consideration interests other than our own, we open ourselves to the idea of selflessness. That, it states, is true enlightenment.

His Holiness, the Dalai Lama, in his book *Essence of the Heart Sutra* discussed compassion in great detail. He writes:

"*According to Buddhism, compassion is an aspiration, a state of mind, wanting others to be free from suffering. It's not passive - it's not empathy alone - but rather an empathetic altruism that actively strives to free others from suffering. Genuine compassion must have both wisdom and loving-kindness. That is to say, one must understand the nature of the suffering from which we wish to free others (this is wisdom), and one must experience deep intimacy and empathy with other sentient beings (this is loving-kindness).*"

In our everyday lives, incorporating compassion means doing good without any expectation of good being done in return. This may seem unrealistic at first, but that is the true compassion that Buddhism gives so much importance to. Expecting a return, even if it is simple appreciation, means not being able to realize the 'we' part. Do we thank ourselves for drinking water? You do something for one another because at the end of the day, we are all one. No thank yous, no debts. This is known as 'Dana Paramita' in Buddhism, which is the perfection of giving. The idea is that giving results in receiving, and therefore, both the parties need each other. How, then, is one superior to the other? That is true compassion.

Buddhism not only teaches you about what compassion is, but also discusses how you can learn, teach, and perfect it. The secret here lies in practice. The first step is to look into oneself and deal with our own demons. By getting rid of our self-delusions, we become more open, more sensitive to what is going on in the world around us.

In Tibetan Buddhism, the concept is known as 'Tonglen.' Pema Chodron, a Buddhist Nun, discusses the issue and claims that Tonglen involves acquainting yourself with your own suffering first, before moving on to develop compassion for others. They are linked, as only after realizing our own suffering do we become capable of understanding others. Tonglen disregards the convention that dictates avoiding suffering in favor of pleasure. Doing so opens us to the true idea of selflessness.

Pema Chodron says,

"*Tonglen reverses the usual logic of avoiding suffering and seeking pleasure and, in the process, we become liberated from a very ancient prison of selfishness. We begin to feel love both for ourselves and others and also we being to take care of ourselves and others. It awakens our compassion and it also introduces us to a far larger view of reality. It introduces us to the unlimited spaciousness that Buddhists call 'shunyata'. By doing the practice, we begin to connect with the open dimension of our being.*"

Buddhism actively stresses that karuna (compassion) without prajna (wisdom) cannot exist, and vice versa. They can only work together toward the realization of true enlightenment.

Conclusion

Having explored the basics of Buddhism, we can finally come up with a plan to incorporate them in our everyday lives. We don't need to be rocket scientists, nor clerics. These principles are extremely simple, and not just for understanding, but also for putting into practice. There's no need to overhaul your entire lifestyle to include what you have learned here. Just by keeping the principles in mind as you go about your daily activities, you will be more aware of the best way to approach or handle the everyday situations you will naturally encounter.

Most of these teachings are ethical considerations that are the basic principles of humanity. They are about love, peace, compassion, and tolerance, all concepts that we have probably been taught from day one. What Buddhism does is take all these principles and combine it into a religion, into a lifestyle of being mindful of opportunities to apply these principles.

Today, people in the West are beginning to look toward Buddhism as an answer to their troubles. The key to whether or not this will work, is whether or not you are willing to exercise the basic principles.

Buddhism is more than just a religion that tells you what to do, but rather it's a lifestyle that anyone can relate to and follow. Buddhism is a symbol of internal peace, bliss, and harmony. And there is good reason for it.

What can enhance these teachings further is learning about the lifestyle of the Great Buddha, who embodied everything he taught. While the basics are explained in this book, there is still a lot more to learn about Buddhism, including the concept of Nirvana, rebirth, and other ideas. But for now, these basic principles should help you mold your life in a way that portrays what you have learned here, and you can start today, right now. But again, there's no need to view this as a major life overhaul – you can even start very small, and focus on making tiny changes, one at a time. Nobody is judging you. This is what Buddhism is all about.

Finally, I'd like to thank you for purchasing this book! If you enjoyed it or found it helpful, I'd greatly appreciate it if you'd take a moment to leave a review on Amazon. Thank you!

Made in the USA
Monee, IL
23 October 2020